COMMUNITY HELPERS

Chefs

by Kate Moening

BLASTOFF! READERS

BELLWETHER MEDIA • MINNEAPOLIS, MN

Note to Librarians, Teachers, and Parents:

Blastoff! Readers are carefully developed by literacy experts and combine standards-based content with developmentally appropriate text.

Level 1 provides the most support through repetition of high-frequency words, light text, predictable sentence patterns, and strong visual support.

Level 2 offers early readers a bit more challenge through varied simple sentences, increased text load, and less repetition of high-frequency words.

Level 3 advances early-fluent readers toward fluency through increased text and concept load, less reliance on visuals, longer sentences, and more literary language.

Level 4 builds reading stamina by providing more text per page, increased use of punctuation, greater variation in sentence patterns, and increasingly challenging vocabulary.

Level 5 encourages children to move from "learning to read" to "reading to learn" by providing even more text, varied writing styles, and less familiar topics.

Whichever book is right for your reader, Blastoff! Readers are the perfect books to build confidence and encourage a love of reading that will last a lifetime!

This edition first published in 2019 by Bellwether Media, Inc.

No part of this publication may be reproduced in whole or in part without written permission of the publisher. For information regarding permission, write to Bellwether Media, Inc., Attention: Permissions Department, 6012 Blue Circle Drive, Minnetonka, MN 55343.

Library of Congress Cataloging-in-Publication Data

Names: Moening, Kate, author.
Title: Chefs / by Kate Moening.
Description: Minneapolis, MN : Bellwether Media, Inc., [2019] | Series:
  Blastoff! Readers: Community Helpers | Audience: Ages 5-8. | Audience: K
  to grade 3. | Includes bibliographical references and index.
Identifiers: LCCN 2018030397 (print) | LCCN 2018032387 (ebook) | ISBN
  9781681036328 (ebook) | ISBN 9781626179011 (hardcover : alk. paper)
Subjects: LCSH: Cooks–Juvenile literature.
Classification: LCC TX652.5 (ebook) | LCC TX652.5 .M635 2019 (print) | DDC
  641.5092–dc23
LC record available at https://lccn.loc.gov/2018030397

Editor: Betsy Rathburn   Designer: Brittany McIntosh

Printed in the United States of America, North Mankato, MN.

Table of **Contents**

Veggie Day

The chef is making soup! She quickly chops vegetables.

The chef puts the veggies into a pot on the stove. Time to cook!

What Are Chefs?

Chefs prepare tasty food! Many work in **restaurants**.

Some chefs make food for big parties. Others are **private** chefs!

What Do Chefs Do?

Chefs decide what goes on the **menu**. They make up **recipes** and buy food.

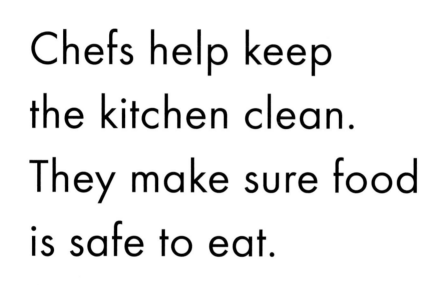

Chefs help keep the kitchen clean. They make sure food is safe to eat.

Chef Gear

food   oven   pan   wooden spoon

Chefs train new cooks. Everyone in the kitchen must know what to do.

What Makes a Good Chef?

Chefs have busy days. They often work late. Chefs must have a lot of **energy**!

Chef Skills

- ✓ good communicators
- ✓ good with details
- ✓ alert
- ✓ energetic

Kitchens have hot ovens and sharp knives. Chefs must be **alert**. Stay safe!

Glossary

alert

quick to notice danger

private

for just one person or group

energy

the power to work or move

recipes

directions for cooking food

menu

a list of meals that people can order, often at a restaurant

restaurants

places where people can buy meals

To Learn More

AT THE LIBRARY

Battista, Brianna. *I Want to Be a Chef.*
New York, N.Y.: PowerKids Press, 2018.

Meister, Cari. *Chefs.* Minneapolis, Minn.:
Bullfrog Books, 2015.

Waldendorf, Kurt. *Hooray for Chefs!*
Minneapolis, Minn.: Lerner Publications, 2017.

ON THE WEB

FACTSURFER

Factsurfer.com gives you
a safe, fun way to find
more information.

1. Go to www.factsurfer.com.

2. Enter "chefs" into the search box.

3. Click the "Surf" button and select your
   book cover to see a list of related web sites.

Index

The images in this book are reproduced through the courtesy of: mangostock, front cover; Pressmaster, pp. 4-5, 6-7; LightField Studios, pp. 8-9; Hero Images/ Getty Images, pp. 10-11; Gorodenkoff, pp. 12-13; style-photo, pp. 14-15; Anna Kucherova, p. 15 (food); little birdie, p. 15 (oven); Pro3DArtt, p. 15 (pan); Maxal Tamor, p. 15 (wooden spoon); Wavebreakmedia/ Getty Images, pp. 16-17; BangkokThai, pp. 18-19; Jacob Lund, pp. 20-21; hxdyl, p. 22 (top left); ESB Professional, p. 22 (middle left); Rawpixel.com, p. 22 (bottom left); JP WALLET, p. 22 (top right); LiliGraphie, p. 22 (middle right); Sorbis, p. 22 (bottom right).